Hens Hop

Written by Michèle Dufresne

PIONEER VALLEY EDUCATIONAL PRESS, INC.

I see a **hen**.
The hen is in a **pen**.

Hens are female chickens.
A group of hens is often
kept in a fenced-in area
called a pen.

3

The hen can hop.

Though they can't fly far, hens use their wings to flap and hop short distances.

I see a hen in the pen.
The pen is hot.

On warm days, hens need water and shade to stay cool and healthy.

7

A hen hid in a **hut**.

Hens like to hide or rest in cozy places, especially when they lay eggs.

A hen got a hug.

glossary

hen

pen

hut